THE AWESOMENESS OF GOD:

HOW HIS MIRACLES AND WONDERS APPLY TO RIGHT-NOW LIVING

by Avis Minott

Copyright ©2020 by Avis Minott

The Awesomeness of God: How His Miracles and Wonders Apply to Right-Now Living By Avis Minott

Printed in the United States of America

All rights reserved solely by the author. The author guarantees all contents are original and do not infringe upon the legal right of any other person or work. No part of this book may be reproduced in any form without the permission of the author.

All Scripture quotations, unless otherwise indicated, are taken from the Holy Bible Amplified Version, Copyright 1962, 1963, 1964, 1977, 1987 by Zondervan Publishing House

Book Cover Artwork by *Sunrai Creations*
Book Formatting by *Visions That Transcend, Inc.*

ISBN 978-0-578-82226-6

DEDICATION

To my beloved husband and friend, who is so humble. His spiritual help, great understanding, encouragement, and love has enlightened me so that I can continue believing in myself—that whatsoever I desire to accomplish; I will do it with a strong faith in God.

To my children: Richard, Sharon, Philip, and their spouses, Desiré, Bob and Denise. And to my grandchildren: Latoya, Philip Jr., and Elizabeth—they have given

. They, too, have helped me in life.

Pastor Dr. Wilson Morales, who own such love to our family, and has given us so much encouragement during difficult times. He continues to keep us in the way of Christ.

To my dear friend, John Scalera, who allowed me to acknowledge his miraculous healing from death to life. He continuously shows his love to my husband and me.

TABLE OF CONTENTS

Foreword: We Owe It All To Jesus vii

Chapter One: God Who Created The Earth, Heavens And All Things 1

Chapter Two: Remembering The Story Of Joseph In The Bible 9

Chapter Three: God's Great Miraculous Works Toward Abraham And Moses 17

Chapter Four: The Faith Of Daniel, Shadrach Meshach, And Abednego 25

Chapter Five: How God Answers Prayers When You Trust And Believe In Him 31

Chapter Six: Miracles Of Jesus And Experiences That Gave Me A Peace In My Heart 43

Chapter Seven: The Raising Of Lazarus And The Miraculous Healing I Experienced 51

Chapter Eight: Never Underestimate The Power Of God 59

Chapter Nine: Be Encouraged, Have Faith That With God, All Things Are Possible 65

Chapter Ten: Sharing Another Experience That Shows The Goodness Of God 85

Chapter Eleven: Past And Present Incidents That Fuels My Faith In God 93

Chapter Twelve: I Give Praise To Our Heavenly Father By Ending With Psalm 8 111

About The Author 115

FOREWORD

We owe it all to Jesus

It has been, and continues to be, a privilege and pleasure as a partaker of the unmistakable hand and providence of God, our Heavenly Father—so gratefully stated in this book.

We have learned to trust the Lord in the difficult times, which everyone experiences by reason of just being alive.

Avis Minott

However, The Master's eyes are always focused on His own, and His eyes, attentive to their cries for help.

What He has done for us, He will do for you also.

Lynden C. Minott,

Husband of the Author

CHAPTER ONE

GOD WHO CREATED THE EARTH, HEAVENS AND ALL THINGS

To whom then will you liken Me, that I should be equal to him? says the Holy One. Lift up your eyes on high and see! Who has created these? He who brings out their host by number and calls them all by name: through the greatness of His might

Avis Minott

and because He is strong in power,
not one is missing or lacks anything.
Isaiah 40:25-26

As I read the book of Genesis in the Bible informing us of how God prepared, formed, and created the heavens and the Earth from empty waste, it touched my heart so much. Darkness was upon the face of the very great deep; the Spirit of God was moving over the face of the waters.

"And God said, 'Let there be light,'; and there was light. God saw that the light was good, and He affirmed and sustained it, and God separated the light from the darkness." Genesis 1:3-4. (Amplified Version)

God also created the birds, animals, wild beasts, and on the sixth day, He formed man from the dust of the ground giving him His breath of life. He created a woman from a rib taken out of the man, both designed in His own image. That is why we are told that we are spirit, soul, and body—when we die, our spirit lives on.

After God made man and woman, He instituted marriage as one man and one woman saying, "Therefore a man shall leave his father and his mother and shall become united and cleave to his wife, and they shall become one flesh." Genesis 2:24. According to the Bible, God created humans so that He can have a relationship with them.

Although He knew our thoughts and rebellions against Him, I sometimes wonder how God created us out of great love.

Have you ever wondered what great disaster would occur on Earth if the sun and moon were ever out of orbit? God controls these two celestial bodies in the sky and everything else in the Universe. People who do not believe in creation always mention Mother Nature, when in fact, God is the one who turns the world on its axis. Consider the creation of the trees, the grass, and their colors. God has made them suitable for our eyesight. I do not think that if He had chosen other colors, our eyes would have been able to focus so naturally. God supplied everything that He knew would be good for us.

I often marvel at the grand notion of conception and life in a woman's body, the joining of egg and sperm, forming a child in a period of nine months. From the time of conception, God allows this child to know when it is time to leave the womb. This baby is fully formed and has developed five senses: feeling, hearing, seeing, tasting, and touching. When these elements connect, a human is formed—yet many will not admit that there is a life inside of a woman at conception. We have aborted so many children, some of whom may have grown to be scientists who could have been able to find cures for many diseases. I can imagine that God, who created us, is so angry that we have taken it upon ourselves to destroy His creations. God's love for us surpassed all understanding when He gave His only Son, Jesus, to die for us while we were yet sinners. He saw how corrupt we would be even before we were formed in our mothers' wombs. But because of His great love for us, He allowed Jesus, who was sinless, to sacrifice His life for us by taking on our sins. We can never fathom the awesomeness of our God.

CHAPTER TWO

REMEMBERING THE STORY OF JOSEPH IN THE BIBLE

Be still and know that I am God …
Psalm 46:10

Remembering the story of Joseph in the Bible is another marvelous occurrence of how God worked in this man's life. As a child, God gave him visions concerning Israel and its role in God's redemption plan. He was so excited about these dreams that he told his brothers. But they refused to believe him, and they mistreated him because of it. Not only did they treat him in this fashion, but also, they had decided to kill him. However, instead, his brothers sold him as a slave to the Egyptians. Joseph was also sent to prison and wrongfully accused of a heinous crime by Potiphar's wife. She told her husband that Joseph tried to rape her. In our reading, right about now, we might ask, *why did Joseph have to endure all these hardships?* But please know that God had a plan for Joseph's life, regardless of these trials and tribulations, and He fulfilled it. Even during the storms, God was always with him.

The Awesomeness Of God

In the end, Joseph became a governor of Egypt and was able to provide for his father and family during the period of great famine. Astonished, his brothers finally asked for forgiveness for everything they had done to him. Joseph explained that even though they meant to cause evil, God turned the situation into something good, showing how God is truly awesome. Look at Genesis, chapters 40-45.

From what occurred, we can see so many lessons to be learned. We should just keep on trusting in God when circumstances look so hopeless that we fear the outcome. If we have a personal relationship with God and live according to how

He says we should, He will do the best for us in His perfect timing. True enough, it scares us sometimes how we have to wait so long for answers, but His answers are so awesome that in time it will make us wonder, *why did we ever worry?*

Again, remember He says, "His ways are not our ways and His thoughts are not our thoughts." (Isaiah 55:8)

When I was back home in Jamaica, feeling rejected by my husband. After being separated for six years, I finally felt that it was time for me to end my marriage officially. I thought that my life would be better, living as a single woman with just my children. And that if it would be the

Lord's Will, at some point in the future, I would be able to find someone with whom I could be happy. Now, I have come to realize that what I had in my mind was not what God had planned for me.

Have you ever read Jeremiah 1:5? It says, "Before I formed you in the womb, I knew you and approved of you, and before you were born, I separated and set you apart, consecrating you and appointed you as a prophet to the nations." This was God speaking to Jeremiah.

We are His children, and I believe He is saying the same thing to us. He wants us to know how special and precious we are to Him.

Again, David wrote in Psalm 139: 15-16, "My frame was not hidden from You, when I was being formed in secret, intricately and curiously wrought in the depths of the earth. Your eyes saw my unformed substance and in Your book all the days of my life were written before ever they took shape when as yet there was none of them."

Experiencing the loss of my marriage caused me to learn so much during that time. But eventually, trusting and having faith in God, He directed me to the right path—in which I was to go. Then, and only then, was I able to see myself just as I was. I asked God for forgiveness. And He taught me how to forgive so many people who had done me wrong in the past. Finally, my understanding was clear, and God made it possible for our children and me to unite with my husband. What a wonderful God we serve!

CHAPTER THREE

GOD'S GREAT MIRACULOUS WORKS TOWARD ABRAHAM AND MOSES

Great is the Lord and highly to be praised in the city of our God! Psalm 48:1

From the great story of Abraham, we should learn how to always have faith in God, regardless of the situation. Because God always fulfills His promises. God told Abraham that He would give him a son through his wife, Sarah. Seeing that she was getting old, Sarah doubted God, and she allowed Abraham to have relations with her handmaid, who became pregnant.

Abraham, now having two sons, one by the handmaid and the other by the promise of Sarah, created a huge division in the family. When you read this story, you will find that Sarah did become pregnant at a very old age during the exact time that God said she would have a son. Isaac, Sarah's son, was born, and then God asked Abraham to give Isaac as an offering to Him. This was a test from God to see how much faith Abraham had in Him.

Abraham's faith was so strong until he believed that God could, and would, bring Isaac back to life. In Abraham's heart, there was no doubt. The awesomeness of this showed greatly when God allowed a lamb to be caught in a thicket for the sacrifice. Only God could do that.

Still, there are times when disobedience to God results in dire consequences. To this day, we are still having wars between the descendants of Abraham's two sons, Ishmael and Isaac. Look at Genesis Chapters 21-22.

Now consider this miracle of God, parting the Red Sea during the time of Moses. God chose him to lead the

Israelites out of Egypt when Pharaoh had to let them go. When they reached the Red Sea, they panicked because they could not move forward. But God told Moses to stretch out his rod over the waters. Instantly, the water parted because the Lord caused the sea to go back by a strong east wind and provided dry ground so they could cross. Then Pharaoh ordered his men to chase after the Israelites to force them back into Egypt. But something miraculous happened; the Lord caused the waters of the sea to fill to return to normal, causing all Pharaoh's men to drown. Look at Exodus14.

The Awesomeness Of God

Sometimes, I find certain situations very hard to overcome, and I ask myself, *why do I have to go through all these things in life?* With so many trials and tribulations, and life challenges, I have often doubted myself—I've doubted some of the life choices I've made. Then, when things go wrong, I wonder if God is chastising me.

But I realize that God wants us to increase our faith. He wants to help us grow stronger in grace, and He wants us to remember that we cannot take on all the burdens we face and solve them without the help of our Lord. The reason why we have such hard times—wondering, fretting, and being overwhelmed—is because we have not taken our burdens to the Lord.

However, we are always to leave our burdens at Jesus' feet and have faith just to let go and ask God to help us. If we can manage that, then we can be at peace in our minds. When we do this, or at least when we work to accomplish this, our load will be lighter. The things that are found to be so difficult will no longer weigh us down and appear to be insurmountable.

While I was writing this, I remembered a time when, some years ago, my husband and I went to Jamaica, our birth home, to visit our families. We were having such a wonderful time, but then came this one horrendous moment, during which I didn't know what to do. In that moment, we were both sleeping, and my husband began choking. His struggle to breathe woke me up. Suddenly, the clock was rapidly ticking between life and death. I just began to call on the name of Jesus.

I can share with you, now, how only the Spirit of God could have told me to do what I did. First, as steadily but as quickly as I could, I helped my husband stand up in front of me. Next, I wrapped my arms around his stomach and squeezed it repeatedly. I squeezed it so much and so many times, refusing to stop until I heard him cough up whatever had him choking. Then, out it flew, and just like that, he was able to breathe again. Only God could have helped me in that situation. Throughout the entire ordeal, I kept repeating to God, "I do not want my husband to die." And God heard my desperate cry.

It is so amazing what God can do if we just trust Him. His love never fails. He wants us to worship Him, praise Him, and thank Him for all that He has done for us. So many had experienced God's wonderful power when Jesus walked the Earth. And He still performs miracles today. Jesus reminds us that He is the same yesterday, today, and forever. He never changes.

CHAPTER FOUR

THE FAITH OF DANIEL, SHADRACH MESHACH, AND ABEDNEGO

The eyes of the Lord are toward the righteous, and His ears are open to their cry.
Psalm 34:15

As I continue sharing, I can remember the story of Daniel. As a child, when my young friends and I went to Sunday School, we were taught about

Daniel in the Lion's Den. But we did not recognize the great magnitude of this great miracle performed by God.

King Belshazzar appointed Daniel to rule over a part of the kingdom. He was discovered worshipping God, even though Darius the King had made a law that whoever worked with him was obligated to worship his pagan gods. Three men saw Daniel praising Jehovah and reported him to the King. When the King heard this report, he was very distressed, and he commanded that Daniel should be put in the den of lions. A stone was laid at the mouth of the den so that Daniel could not get out. He was left there overnight, but God sent His angels to shut the lions' mouths to protect Daniel.

In the morning, when Darius came to the den, believing that Daniel was dead, he got a surprise.

Daniel called out to him and said, "O king live forever."

Can you imagine the expression on the King's face when he saw Daniel alive? This is the God we serve. He is the One who has great power to do anything.

What about the three Jewish men: Shadrach, Meshach, and Abednego, who were thrown in the fiery furnace but came out completely unburned. They had faith that God would deliver them. King Nebuchadnezzar wanted them to worship his gods and to bow down to his golden image. But they refused.

The King became so furious; he ordered that they be placed in the fiery furnace. He also commanded that the furnace be heated seven times hotter. And he then sent for the strongest men in his army to bind them. These Babylonian army men were well-attired for the effects of this searing, deadly heat. However, as they went to throw the Hebrew men—Shadrach, Meshach, and Abednego—in the furnace, the heat was so extremely hot that they, themselves, were killed. These three Hebrew men went into that furnace, and they knelt and prayed. God showed up in that fiery furnace.

Later, when the King finally opened the furnace, he was dumbfounded when he saw four men instead of three. Then he called out to his men and said, "I saw four men loosed walking in the midst of the fire not hurt, and the fourth looks like the Son of God." Once again, God showed how awesome He is. Look at Daniel 3:12-30.

These stories have given me so much more courage to continue serving the Lord. It is also wise for us to continue to allow ourselves to be guided by God's words so that we will not fear when we are faced with circumstances that attack us. So often, we find ourselves in the midst of dire situations that we are not equipped to handle alone. Our only true recourse is for us to trust in the Lord because He sees and knows everything and what we need.

CHAPTER FIVE

HOW GOD ANSWERS PRAYERS WHEN YOU TRUST AND BELIEVE IN HIM

Lean on, trust in and be confident in the Lord with all your heart and mind and do not rely on your own understanding, in all your ways recognize and acknowledge Him and He will direct Your path.

Proverbs 3:5-6

Avis Minott

My husband, Lynden, and I worked and lived in New York City for more than thirty years. Finally came the time for his retirement, and we pondered how to take on the next journey of our years. Should we return to our birth home, Jamaica, or stay in the United States. As we were carefully coming to our decision to remain in the U.S., we were offered a choice to live in Maryland, where our daughter lived.

I went into prayer for months just to find out what God would have us to do. Yes, it was a hard decision to make. But I just felt that God would help us. We knew that financially, living in Jamaica would be best for us because we had a home there, mortgage-free. Our only expenses would have been to pay utilities. However, after hearing reports of brutal attacks on repatriating Jamaicans, we became frightened. Hearing about such violence, we felt that returning to Jamaica would not be a good idea. In addition to that, all our children were here in the states. And none of them had any intentions of returning to Jamaica. So, we thought it best to remain in the United States and sell the house we owned in Jamaica.

Now, the time came to think about where we would live. We knew that we would probably purchase a house either in

New York or Maryland. And let me say, here, that prayer is a wonderful thing to do when you're in doubt. After submitting that dilemma to prayer, my daughter soon gave me a wonderful idea. She suggested that we first come to Maryland, where she lived with her family, to see if we would like the area. We usually spent time with our daughter, her husband, and her daughter during special occasions and vacations. But now, we would visit her because we were on a special mission.

I just knew this was God's answer to our decision because the exact day we came to Maryland to visit, there was a house for sale near my daughter's home. But I

The Awesomeness Of God

still was not totally sure, though, if this was what Lynden and I should do. Still, we decided to find out if we could take a look at the house. We were told it had just gone on the market that exact day and the only way we could see it was if we had a real estate agent. It had not been shown to anyone yet, and it was not a certainty that we could purchase it until it was shown to others. My daughter was able to give me her friend's name, who was an agent. Soon after, we finally had an opportunity to inspect the house. We submitted a bid.

We went home to New York in the interim, and we just left it in God's hands. I told Lynden that if we did not get it that

that would be fine with me. "I trust God for the right decisions," I told him. I just had so much faith in God that He would do the best for us.

One week after seeing the house, we got a call from the real estate agent. The agent let us know that if we desired the house, "It's yours," she said.

I just kept praising God and thanking Him for making this decision possible. We went through all the processing of papers and the checking of our credit, and by the help of God, we were approved. For the down payment, we wondered if we would be able to come up with the money.

The Awesomeness Of God

When our credit was checked, by God's help, the bank told us that our credit was very good, and we did not have to give a down payment, only a closing cost. A few days before the closing date, a check came in the mail for more than the amount we needed to pay. When we sent a check to pay the real estate agency, we got another surprise. We were given an unexpected refund. Plans were made, and we were able to move to Southern Maryland.

God had done this for us, which was not a surprise because I know that all things are possible with Him. His words are *to seek His Kingdom first, and all things will be added unto us.* Also, if we trust in

Him and have faith, He will allow everything to fall into place—in His timing. I am not saying that this is easy to do. But, in faith, we must at least seek to go through the testy waters first. Sometimes, we must go through the fire to meet the flames. But God will go through it all with us. We have been here, living in Maryland for sixteen years, and there has been no regret. The church we attend is *Encounter Christian Center* in Charlotte Hall, where God has placed us to do His work until He calls us home or until Jesus' return. Always remember to let go and let God. This was yet another area of my life in which the awesomeness of God was proven.

The Awesomeness Of God

Not too long ago, I experienced the awesomeness of God again. And even now, whenever I think on it, there is such a level of simplicity, yet exactness, to it—meant just for me—that it is still so unbelievable. I went to the store to purchase an item. Its posted price was $7.99. I was a bit short on cash to purchase the item, so I decided to go another route and use my debit card. I preferred paying cash, but I needed the item badly. I went up to the cash register with the item, and the clerk swiped the barcode. Surprisingly, the cash register valued the product for eleven cents. I had expected it to cost around five dollars. The clerk and I were dumbfounded, so she erased what she had rung up and started the ringing-up process anew. She did it twice more; the same amount came up. I only paid eleven cents for the item. And I *did* pay cash. At that moment, all I could say was, "Thank you, Jesus." I realized that God had worked a miracle on my behalf. I knew it was God because He has always shown me what He can do.

Looking back on my life, even up until now, I can say that I would never do anything differently because God has blessed my husband and me so much—since we decided to be obedient to His Word. I know I am not perfect, but God has changed me so tremendously that now my only concern is to help others and to forgive others who should be forgiven. I have learned so much spiritually. Ever since I wrote my first book, titled, *From Birth to New Birth*, the peace that God has given me is amazing. And even though life still has its ups and downs—do know that we have been through a lot in recent years—I just keep on trusting in God. It is the most triumphant way to live.

CHAPTER SIX

MIRACLES OF JESUS AND EXPERIENCES THAT GAVE ME A PEACE IN MY HEART

I will praise you, O Lord, with my whole heart, I will show all Your marvelous works and wonderful deeds. Psalm 9:1

When Jesus came into the world, He performed so many miracles through the power of God; it marveled many people.

His first miracle was turning water into wine. Jesus and His mother, Mary, attended a wedding in Cana of Galilee. At the wedding, they ran out of wine, so Mary told Jesus what had occurred. She knew that her Son would be able to do something good about this, so she told the servants at the wedding to do whatever Jesus told them to do. Jesus directed them to fill six waterpots with water. As they poured the water, it slowly turned into wine which was unbelievable to everyone who witnessed this miracle. Look at John 2:1-10.

Also, another miracle was when Jesus went to a town called Bethsaida, where he was teaching, and many people followed Him. His disciples came to Him when it was getting late and told Him to send the people away. Jesus, seeing that they were hungry, told them to give the people some food to eat. They told Him that all they had was five loaves and two fishes. The number of people who were present was about 5,000 men. Jesus had them sit in groups which they did. He then took the five loaves and two fishes, looked up to heaven, praised God, and gave thanks, and He asked for blessings on the food. He broke them and gave His disciples to place before the multitude. All the people ate and were satisfied, and after eating, twelve baskets of broken pieces remained. How can we not trust a God who loves us so much?

In other instances, Lynden and I have often gone to a restaurant to eat, and before we could get around to paying for our food, someone would come to our table and pay our check. I wonder at times why we worry so much, especially when God has everything under control. He knows everything about us. And even before we can get around to asking Him for anything, He answers. It is time we all exercise the faith God has given us and just wait on Him. I include myself in that line of direction, too.

The Awesomeness Of God

There once was a time when I found myself worrying so much that my head would hurt. Now I know to just keep on praying when the trials of life come. Finally, I learned to ask God for His help to not be that way, to not drown myself in worry. Basically, I was asking Him for a change. And God answered my prayer.

Oddly enough, He showed me, one evening, while I went shopping. I had been parked at a restaurant and was prepared to drive off. But while I was sitting in my car with my mind consumed with worry over one thing and then another, the car beside mine suddenly spun away. The car's roaring engine jolted me out of my thoughts in time to see its bumper sticker that brandished as big as day, *Let Go and let God*. Immediately, I realized that God was sending me a message. He wanted me to break out of that suffocating web.

I released my anxiety, sat back, and said, "Thank You, Lord." I then began to praise the Lord, and it was at that time when I remembered that God had spoken to me many times before, telling me to just leave everything to Him. That occurred about a year ago, and I can still say that God has given me such a peace in my heart that I just have to keep on the positive side of concentrating on God. I have no choice but to keep believing that with

The Awesomeness Of God

Him, all things are possible. I thank God so much, and every day, for showing me how awesome He is. And for showing me that all we have to do is to believe in Him.

CHAPTER SEVEN

THE RAISING OF LAZARUS AND THE MIRACULOUS HEALING I EXPERIENCED

*Praise the Lord give thanks to the
Lord, for He is good:
For His mercy and loving kindness
endure forever. Psalm 106:1*

Have you read in the Bible how Jesus brought Lazarus back to life? It was told that he was dead for four days and had started to decay. Jesus spoke to God, His Father, went to the tomb and called Lazarus to come forth. Lazarus immediately rose from the dead and came out of that tomb. Everyone marveled at the miracle Jesus performed. John11:38-44. The story of Lazarus brings my attention to a great miracle my husband and I experienced that was centered on a very dear friend of ours.

About three years ago, our friend who lives very close to us in Waldorf, Maryland, and whom we usually meet up with during the summer gave us a great shock. One day, he called to ask us to meet with him. We were unable to go with him at the moment, so we told him we would call him when we found the time. The following week, when we tried to reach him, we got no reply. Then his sister called the following day, telling us that she had tried to get a hold of him, too. But he was not answering his phone.

"I found your telephone number," she explained, "in a list, my brother gave to me."

"We'll go over to check his house to make sure he's okay," we assured our friend's sister. We then drove to his house that Monday afternoon, about 3 p.m., and we realized that something was wrong as we parked the car even before we walked up to his home. His garden, which was always kept clean, was completely overgrown with grassy weeds and shrubs. We knocked on the front door for at least twenty minutes before he came to open it. Finally, he came to the door badly disheveled and in tears. We were aghast as he struggled to tell us about the pain in his head.

We pushed ourselves in, holding him up and asking if he'd had anything to eat.

"No," he said.

We realized he needed to be taken to the hospital. Lynden called his sister in North Carolina to give her the details. She, in turn, called her other brother, who was about an hour and a half away from us. He said he would be there by about 4:00 p.m. While waiting for him, I made our friend a cup of coffee and something for him to eat. Struggling, he drank a few sips of coffee. He was in so much pain, he couldn't keep still, and he couldn't eat. Lynden and I tried our best to calm and settle him, hoping to ease his pain.

When his brother arrived, he took one look at him and called 911 immediately. Understandably, he moved so fast, we all barely had enough time to greet one another. The situation grew more intensely dire by the minute. Finally, the ambulance came and rushed him to the hospital. We all jumped in our respective cars and rushed there as well. After an immediate triage, our friend had to be transported by helicopter to the Georgetown Hospital in Washington, D.C.

The doctor at the first hospital said to us all, "If he had stayed one minute longer without medical attention, he would have been a dead man."

Our friend had immediate surgery because he had been hemorrhaging in his brain for about a week's worth of time. After surgery, he was in a comatose condition for about two more weeks.

Unbelievably so, he is still alive today. Our friend is still staying strong—working and praising God to be alive. And besides this miracle of sustained life, God made it so that neither could he remember anything about the day we found him nor could he recall the horrific pain he had suffered. God sent us to his aid at the exact correct time—not when our friend wanted us to visit, but when he needed our help the most. We serve an awesome God, and we should be praising him daily. Our friend is praising God every day for his life.

CHAPTER EIGHT

NEVER UNDERESTIMATE THE POWER OF GOD

*I will extol You my God, O King and
I will bless Your name forever and
ever. Psalm 145:1*

Well, it's been a long time since I have written anything, so that's why I decided to pen another spiritual memoir. So many things have occurred that I decided to take time to share more experiences which have been blessings to me.

Before sharing my other experiences, a thought came to my mind concerning our Lord and Savior Jesus Christ. It was an awesome act of God, our Father, had done when He sent Jesus to die on the cross for us. Saving us from condemnation, and through Jesus' resurrection, we are made alive in Him—able to have a personal relationship with the Father and Son. This causes me to think of the wonderful love God has for us. As His children, we should love others just as He loves us. And what a wonderful world this would be if we would all follow in Jesus' way. The price that He paid for us by giving His life was magnificent. Because of this, we are saved from sin by His grace and death on the cross. Look at John 20:1-10.

One Wednesday afternoon at about noon, I was accosted by two men while in the Walmart Shopping Center. First, they came with a leather-like billfold with money, purposely visible, asking me if I would share it with them. But first, they wanted me to give them a ride to a specific place. Immediately, God showed me that they would rob me and cause me bodily harm if I went with them. After that, I was able to get away from them and quickly drive away. Only God could have helped me in that situation—because everything happened so fast without warning.

Another incident occurred three days later. I was invited to a birthday party. Driving, as I searched for a parking space close to my destination, I was unsuccessful. Unbeknownst to me, the space I was able to find harbored a healthy patch of mud. My vehicle got stuck. I was not that far from the house where the celebration was taking place, but it was still an uncomfortable walk away—and now my car was stuck. Deciding to switch gears to look for another space, I could not get my car to budge. The engine raced, the tires worked to spin themselves out, but it was a losing battle. Not knowing quite what to do, I then said, "Lord, I need your help."

Next, I was making a move to get out of the car and begin my trek to the house where the party was being held. Immediately, a man in a truck seemingly came from nowhere. I didn't even get the chance to hear or see another vehicle approaching my car. The man hopped out of the truck, greeted me, friendly-like, attached my car to his truck, and pulled it right out.

With a smile, the man said, "You are okay now."

"Thank you so much," I said to him, "God bless you."

"I saw you in trouble, and I came to help," he simply responded.

And I'm not exaggerating when I say that I had no clue from where he had come, and I do not know where the man went after he so graciously helped me, either. In that moment, God had sent help.

Entering the home, I told everyone what had taken place. They all asked why I did not call them, but I was so excited to tell them how this man came to my rescue. As always, God answered my prayer.

CHAPTER NINE

BE ENCOURAGED, HAVE FAITH THAT WITH GOD, ALL THINGS ARE POSSIBLE

Be strong and let your heart take courage, all you who wait for and hope for and expect the Lord.
Psalm 31:24

These past incidents, I'm sharing now, have come to mind, and I would like to include them before I close this—my inspirational pocket guide memoir—which is my encouragement to you and my tribute to God.

About in 1985, my husband and I purchased a house in Mount Vernon, New York. We lived there for about fifteen years. In that course of time, our children had matured and had moved on to live their own lives. But, of course, that is the natural progression of things. Birdies must leave the nest to fly. But it left us alone in a big house.

So, we decided to rent a part of the house to tenants. And for a few years, it had been a favorable and lucratively sustaining solution. But then, as time went on, conditions began to deteriorate. The tenants were not living up to their responsibilities of paying their rent. The two young ladies, we discovered, were on drugs. We found this out when we spied small packets thrown around in the yard and on our home's sidewalk. We were told that if those small packets, filled with drugs, were found by the police, we would surely lose our home. So, we had to give them notice to leave.

The tenants left, owing a few months' rent that left us still paying a mortgage without receiving the needed rental income. We also had to supply heat during the New York winter. This situation was extremely hard on us. I could not ask our children for help because they were young and just starting life for themselves. They had their own families to take care of. So, we just had to do what we could do.

During this time, my husband became very ill. I worked as a Travel Consultant in Manhattan. I had clients who came and purchased, on credit, air tickets to travel and promised to pay up when they returned. But they never did. So, I found myself with ten thousand dollars of debt. We then refinanced the mortgage to pay off our debts. We felt that we could maintain our home from what we had left. However, this did not work out because our earnings were not enough to carry us through. Our last resort was to sell the house. But time was running out on that idea. Things got so bad we decided to go the bankruptcy route.

We started proceedings, but God spoke to us about how it was not right for us as Christians to not pay our bills. We canceled the proceedings and decided to trust in Him. Eventually, foreclosure came upon us, and we were forced to give up our home. I was very sad because I knew that God had helped us to get our home. I also felt that perhaps foreclosure had happened to us because I had made promises to God that I had not kept. When I made this purchase, I promised God that I would turn the attic into a prayer room. I got the house. I got the attic, but I was faulty on making it a prayer room. Thus, I was not praying consistently in the way that I should have.

Throughout this entire situation, my husband's illness worsened. In the midst, we had to find a place to rent. Also, I needed to be close to Lynden, so I had to leave my job in Manhattan. We kept praying and trusting in God. We were able to find an apartment in Mount Vernon that was a very reasonable rental. Of course, it was much smaller than where we lived before, but we just had to adjust to this environment. The only person who lived at this place was an older man of German descent, and he was so polite. We remained friends for many years until his recent death. We were so sorry when we received the news.

Leaving my job in Manhattan was what God wanted me to do; I know that. Long before I was forced to leave the job because of my husband's health, I had intentions of doing so. But even while our situation was mandating it, I was lacking the nerve to make a move. That was until an elderly lady at my church told me about a vision that had come to her. She told me how God was telling her that I should leave my job. She told me this, not knowing how much I had wanted to make a change. Manhattan was just too big of a daily commute—and then came Lynden's illness. God used that woman to confirm my feelings and to give me the nerve I needed to push me into action.

I then began my search for a job in the area where I lived. It wasn't long before I met a man, planning to start a travel agency. Because I was qualified with all my licenses and certificates in this field, he said he would appoint me as his company manager. Not only did he want me to help him, but also, he needed me. This man had no knowledge of the business. Everything went smoothly until he got approved, got his own license, and then employed a young woman to work with me. The first hiccup was that I was unaware of this woman being much closer to my boss than a mere employee. She would not take instructions from me, probably because she didn't have to, and there were so many problems that arose because of it. Finally, I left the job. Soon after, this lady was fired because she had stolen a lot of money from the airlines—money that the travel agency had to repay. All in all, the business went down. Some years later, after that entire ordeal, that same man died.

I went to another travel agency to work. After being there for one year, an

FBI investigator came to the office one evening, asking questions about my boss. Only God was my protector through this time. I did not know that the woman for whom I worked was a thief. It turned out that she was a wanted fugitive for stealing money from both airlines and clients. But until that moment, the moment she had set up a new operation, the FBI could not find her.

Can you imagine? I was her assistant manager. I should have known with whom I was working. Or at least I should have been able to catch on to her dirty dealings. More importantly, it could have been a fair assumption by the FBI that I would indeed know something. Perhaps, the FBI could have assumed that I was working alongside her in her dirty dealings. But she had kept me in the dark, perhaps for the simple reason of not wanting to share any of her ill-gotten gains. However, none of that kept many people from calling me for refunds or displaying their anger over the situation. It was one terrible ordeal. To this day, I cannot understand how God got me through all that. But He did.

Eventually, I decided to open my own agency. And thank God, it was a good decision. During this time, I stayed close to God. I kept on praying, and I was also given a deaconess position in the church

I attended. Spiritually, I loved what I was doing. But Satan started disruption in the church. It was bad. It had gotten so bad until the pastor became very ill. The church broke up, the sheep scattered, and my husband and I left the church as well. Now we began to search for a new church home. We spent some time at two churches, but we never became comfortable enough to make either church our church home. Finally, we began worshipping at the Assemblies of God Church in White Plains, New York. This was the best decision we had made in many years. Financially, though, we were not doing good. We had so many bills to pay, but by the grace of God, He intervened. Leaving that first job in Manhattan was still the best thing I had done because my husband was healed.

I then began to pray fervently to God concerning our financial situation. During this time, I actually heard a voice saying to me, "Give a donation to *CBN* [the Christian Broadcasting Network]."

I could not understand this. We were paying our tithes at church, though not regularly, because we had no church for a time, and there were times when we just could not find enough money to do so. But I was obedient to the Word, and I started giving twenty dollars each month to *CBN*. It was unbelievable how money suddenly began coming to us from different avenues—avenues upon which we had not anticipated or had present knowledge of. Slowly but surely, my business was growing. My husband was getting refund checks from his job. And it just went on like that.

Once, the bank said it had made an error in our account and returned an amount that we neither missed nor expected to receive. We could not understand what was happening. So, I started a savings account, something we hadn't been able to do beforehand. God helped us so much that we paid off all our bills. We became debt-free, and we were also able to increase our donations to *CBN*.

Recently I went to the supermarket to do my monthly shopping. I had decided before going there to do other things like paying a few bills, going to the post office to buy stamps as I usually do each month, and going to the bank to make deposits. However, as I sat in the car contemplating what I should do first, I thought that I should do the other items first and then do the shopping last. I do not know why this thought came to me because each month, I usually do my shopping early in the morning to avoid contact with so many people in the supermarket since the COVID-19 Global Pandemic.

I was a little hesitant when the thought came to me, and I asked the Lord, saying, "God, I do not know what to do at this moment, but You know the best thing for me to do. So, I ask for Your direction." I talk to God often when I am in doubt. And it seemed as if God said to do the shopping last. So, I did.

I went in the supermarket with my list and started getting all my items together, checking the prices as I go along to see that I do not go over my budget. After finishing, I then got into a line where others were waiting to be checked. I was waiting a long time because the two persons before me had fully packed carts. I decided to move to a much shorter line, but something in my spirit said, *stay where you are.* As my time came for me to check my groceries, taking them out of the cart, the cashier politely asked, "How was your day today?"

I joyfully replied to her, "Thank God, I am doing fine, and He has blessed me so much that I have to give Him thanks."

As my groceries were being checked, I saw a lady standing in front of the cashier outside, where the groceries were being bagged. She was also speaking to the cashier, so I thought she was a friend or family member. Groceries all checked out; I looked at the total, brandishing $125.00. When I took out my debit card to pay the bill, the cashier took my card and said, "This lady beside me is paying for your groceries."

I was dumbfounded, and all I could say was, "Thank you so much, and God bless you!" I do not know how many times I repeated what I said because I was in shock. Then a little while after, I said, "God has blessed me again because I have blessed so many people, too."

God is good, isn't He? How could I not serve Him? He has done so much for me. Perhaps, right now, you might be in a place where I once was. Be encouraged and serve God, who is your Creator. Do not give up. God has a purpose for each one of us. And it is on us; it's a part of our life's journey to find out what that purpose is. This is why I pray so much. It's because I know God answers prayer. At times there have been things for which I have asked the Lord, and He did not answer in the way that I had anticipated. But I've learned to simply leave everything to Him. I know that if my prayers align with God's Will, that fruitful answers will arrive in the perfect timing. God is never late. There are things that, as a human being, I still have to work on. As long as I am in my flesh, I will never be perfect. But God is still teaching me to be humble and to continue trusting in Jesus, my Lord.

CHAPTER TEN

SHARING ANOTHER EXPERIENCE THAT SHOWS THE GOODNESS OF GOD

Yet grace was given to each of us individually, but in different ways in proportion to the measure of Christ's gift. Ephesians 4:7

This is another amazing incident that occurred about five years ago when my husband and I went shopping at a store. Leaving the store and approaching our vehicle, a woman beckoned to us from her SUV. It was parked close to the store. She called out to us, asking us to come and pray for her and her family, who was with her in her vehicle. We had never seen this woman prior to this, and quite frankly, we put the question to her, "Why did you call on us?"

She then confirmed that when we stepped out of the store, she saw a shining light over us that drew her to the conclusion that we were indeed servants of God. She also said to us, "You will not be seeing me again."

We stopped in our tracks and prayed for her. Since that encounter, I have wondered even more about the awesomeness of God in our lives. He knew that this woman needed prayer at that moment, and He allowed us to minister to her.

In the writing of this incident, I'm remembering Paul the Apostle, who was a persecutor of Christians. Regardless, the Lord Jesus used him to bring the words of salvation to the Gentiles when God's people, the Jews, would not accept Jesus and the Gospel.

I cannot understand why I remembered the Apostle Paul at this moment, but his conversion was amazing. The story of Apostle Paul was meant to show that

God's grace is sufficient for us in our times of need. This lady was in need of help, and God intervened.

We may never know the full extent of the way that we should go and what God can accomplish in us.

Do you remember how Paul became a follower of God? The story was told of how Paul was traveling to Damascus, having a murderous desire against the disciples of God, when suddenly a light flashed around him. He was thrown to the ground, and he heard a voice saying to him, "Why are you persecuting me?"

At this moment, Paul knew it was the Lord speaking to him, and immediately his reply was, "Who are you, Lord?"

And He answered him saying, "I am Jesus whom you are persecuting. It is dangerous, and it will turn out badly for you to keep kicking against the goad (to offer vain and perilous resistance)."

Trembling and astonished, Paul asked Jesus what he desired of him. From this, we can see that if you are a child of God, anyone who tries to harm you or do anything to you—because you are a follower of Christ—they are also persecuting God. Jesus directed Paul to go to Damascus because of him being blinded by God; the men who followed him had to lead him. Paul's life was transformed from his corruption into becoming a servant of God. I thank God for his wonderful teachings in the Bible that brought us to salvation. Look at Acts 9:1-43.

God knows who he wants to use in any circumstance; therefore, we should always be spiritually prepared for His surprises. This also teaches us to always pray for anyone doing evil because God can change them. Admittedly, such a thing is very hard to do because some of us can do such terrible things to one another—and without remorse.

The Awesomeness Of God

But still, there are so many stories in the Bible that proves the awesomeness of our God. If we would only trust Him and follow His lead, what a great and wonderful world this would be.

CHAPTER ELEVEN

PAST AND PRESENT INCIDENTS THAT FUELS MY FAITH IN GOD

Now faith is the assurance of things hoped for being the proof of things we do not see and the conviction of their reality. Hebrews 11:1

I could never complete this memoir, *The Awesomeness of God*—my word of encouragement to you—without mentioning another experience I had while visiting my family in Mountain Side, St. Elizabeth in Jamaica, West Indies. It was a Sunday morning, I decided to go to church, and afterward, I would return to Kingston on the eastern side, where I was staying. That morning, I got dressed and went to my car only to realize that my gas tank was showing empty. I then realized that on this day, all the gas stations were closed. When my brother, who was with me, grew frantic about the situation, I prayed in my heart. Then I told him that since we had time, let us go to Black River (which was eight miles from home) to see if a gas station might be open.

"I do not think you'll find any gas stations open," my brother said, "in all our towns, all of the gas stations are closed on this day." He also wondered how I would manage to reach, even a closed gas station, "with an empty tank."

I do not know how or where I got the faith to say to him, "My God will fill my gas tank."

We started on the journey, and a few minutes away, the needle went up to a little over a quarter tank. I beckoned to my brother to take a look at the needle.

Shocked, he said, "No, I do not believe this!" he exclaimed. Still staring at the needle on the dial, he said, "maybe it was stuck."

Anyway, we arrived at Black River, and thank God, a gas station was open. So, we filled the tank. We then returned home, went to church, and had a wonderful blessing.

Unbelievably, the preacher started his message, and the first thing he said was, "Has anyone had the experience of God filling your gas tank?" He then told his experience of God filling his gas tank.

I was speechless. I looked at my brother, and he also could not believe what the preacher had said. But it was just confirmation of what had occurred to us. God had filled our gas tank, too.

You might be in a difficult position with nowhere to turn, and you do not know what to do. Have faith in God.

Believe He can make the impossible possible, and He will surprise you with what He can do for you. Never underestimate the power of our Father. He is the greatest. So, I continue to say, only trust Him because He is awesome.

A few months ago, I was sitting in my car in my church's parking lot when something caught my attention. It was a beautiful winter's day, and I had found myself gazing at the trees, studying their branches minus their leaves. The thought came to me about how God says He is the vine, and we are the branches. My mind's eye started to develop, showing me that God is the vine (the tree without branches). He made us in His image (we are the branches) to be connected to Him. Being attached, we should be like Him, talk like Him, think like Him, and follow His direction. But it is so sad when not all of us choose to follow in His path. Such a choice is the reason why we are so messed up in life. But because of His matchless love for us, He is so awesome to forgive us for all our failures. And God still recognizes us as His

The Awesomeness Of God

children—if we believe in His Son, Jesus, sent to die on a cross for us.

I could continue on and on, giving all the experiences in my life and in the lives of others, proving God's awesome intervention. But, I tell you that those examples would never end.

Now, I know that some of you might ask that if this is so, why are there so many people who are not healed or have not been given second chances, and why do they die when they do? Only God has those infinite answers. We will never understand God's reasons for everything that happens on this Earth. However, all we have to do is thank Him for all He has done for us and encourage others to keep a good heart, be faithful to Him, and to stay in His Word. And He will strengthen our hearts.

I'm hopeful that whatever I have been inspired to write will be of great help and encouragement to anyone who finds his or her way to this pocket guide of love. If you have not accepted the Lord yet, as your personal Savior, I would advise you to think about what you have read and to turn your life over to your Creator, who loves you so much. If you know Him personally, dedicate your life fully to Him and make Him the center of your life. God is to be glorified.

God's Intervention — In Progress

Even at the printing of this inspirational pocket guide memoir, God has shown me another pathway to faith in Him. While watching a movie based on someone's real-life experience, it came to me that perhaps, I could use this to share encouragement to anyone who is experiencing fear and failures, as well as pondering the question *Why should these things happen to me?*

The show began with a young teenager (we'll call her Mary), who lived with one parent, her father, after her mother had died. They were both believers of God and could always be seen praying together. At her school, she was very good in her chosen sport, ice skating. But when the time came for her to compete with others, she became very nervous and believed she would not be able to win. There was another teenager who was in her class who was also good. This girl was confident that even if she and Mary both entered the same competition, she would win the first prize for the school. The competition was set to happen soon as the movie progressed forward.

Eventually, the time came for them to compete with other schools, and they both were chosen to enter the competition. Their coaches did do a great job, preparing them both for a win—after all, everyone wanted to bring in a victory for the school. On the day of the competition, they all performed, and Mary was the one who won the first prize. She was so surprised that she had become the winner. Stunned and elated, Mary got into her car and drove off, heavily distracted by the event of the day. Mary was speeding. And it wasn't long before she lost control of the car and crashed it into a tree. She was thrown out of the car, suffering head and body injuries, and deemed in a critical state.

After being in the hospital for a few days, she revived and was healed from her injuries. The doctor told her father how he had seen a few patients who had been in the kind of accident that Mary had experienced and even suffered similar injuries. No one had ever survived, the doctor expressed. Mary had a limp on her right side and slight memory loss. The doctor told her father that she would need some therapy to get back in the right state of mind. But he would not say that she would be able to skate again—the thing she loved doing.

The doctor advised her father to take her to a certain therapy organization that used horses for helping children and adults. The therapist at this organization was a young man who had helped Mary so much, and during the times she spent there, he became interested in her. The owner of the organization was very upset about this and reprimanded him about their relationship.

In the meantime, the girl who had lost the competition at the school began to say bad things about Mary, and this girl's father, who happened to be a high official in the town, visited the organization to warn the officials there that he would allow their license to be taken away if they did not stop treating Mary. I think this girl was jealous of Mary getting better. Perhaps if Mary regained her health, the girl feared that she would never be able to beat Mary in a future competition.

After a few days in therapy, Mary decided to try to see if she could skate, but unfortunately, she could not gain her balance or any of her former luster. Mary grew very frustrated and began crying to her dad. She asked him, "Dad why did God allow this to happen to me?"

Her dad replied, "I could not tell you why. Also, I cannot tell you why your mom died, but you just have to trust God."

The therapist did not give up on Mary, and she improved rapidly. But she still was not able to skate. She then decided to think of another career that would be of interest to her when she left school. Because of her great improvement, she got very interested in what this company did, and Mary decided to study in that direction. Now she wanted to become a therapist to help other people like herself.

What she said, while growing into that change of thought, caught my attention, and that is why I decided to add this to my writing. Her remarks were, "If I do not get the opportunity to skate again, I will do something else because I can feel something good will come out of this decision."

Then I remembered this scripture from the Bible, "We are assured and know that ... all things work together and are ... for good to and for those who love God and are called according to His design and purpose." Romans 8:28 (AMP)

To end this story, the film continued by showing us how after five years, this same girl, Mary, and the therapist who fell in love with her, had gotten married and opened their own therapy business. Now their main purpose was to help children and adults, which became a great success.

I wonder what would you say about our God? Are you experiencing difficulties and uncertainties that you are trying to get through? And is it also true that these are difficulties beyond your understanding?

The Awesomeness Of God

Why is this happening to you? You ponder. Go to God. He is our only source. He will comfort and give you rest.

It also came to my memory, this song by Joe Ligon and *Mighty Clouds of Joy* that I used to sing years ago:

> I came to Jesus as I was,
>
> I was weary, worn and sad
>
> I found in Him a resting place
>
> And He has made, made me glad …

I'm hopeful that this will be an encouragement to you—all who will read these few words I have written today.

CHAPTER TWELVE

I GIVE PRAISE TO OUR HEAVENLY FATHER BY ENDING WITH PSALM 8

1   O LORD our Lord, how excellent is Your name in all the earth, You have set Your glory above the heavens.

2   Out of the mouth of babes and un-weaned infants, You have established strength because of Your foes, that You might silence the enemy and the avenger.

Avis Minott

3   When I view and consider Your heavens, the work of Your fingers, the moon and the stars, which You have ordained and established;

4   What is man that You are mindful of him? And the son of man, that You care for him?

5   Yet You have made him but a little lower than the angels, and You have crowned him with glory and honor.

6   You made him to have dominion over the works of Your hands: You have put all things under his feet:

7   All sheep and oxen, yes, and the beast of the field;

8   The birds of the air, and the fish of the sea, and whatever passes along the paths of the seas.

9   O Lord our Lord, how excellent is Your name in all the earth!

The Amplified Version

About the Author

Avis Minott, Jamaican-born of mixed culture, was brought up in an English way of living, as was the custom in Jamaica during the 20th Century. Her stepfather, Gustavus Canegan, who was of Irish descent, was very strict, well-spoken, and was an Inspector of Police. As a result, she had to speak perfect English and follow all the principles of good etiquette. Minott became a Christian at the age of twenty-two years old when she attended the Billy Graham

Crusade in Jamaica, 1958. She got married to Lynden Minott on February 21, 1960. Together, living in Southern Maryland, they've been blessed with three children and three grandchildren.

Minott, a member of the *Life Journeys Writers Guild, Inc.*, is most hopeful that this pocket guide memoir of encouragement will be a great blessing to everyone who reads it—and that each reader will experience *The Awesomeness of God*.

www.ingramcontent.com/pod-product-compliance
Lightning Source LLC
Chambersburg PA
CBHW051405290426
44108CB00015B/2156